somewhere

there's a horse

somewhere there's a horse

Ron Wallace

Photo Credit – Cullen Whisenhunt

Text copyright © 2026 by Ron Wallace
All Rights Reserved. Printed in the United States of America

Published by Motina Books, LLC, Bailey, CO
www.MotinaBooks.com

Library of Congress Cataloguing-in-Publication Data:

Names: Wallace, Ron
Title: Somewhere There's a Horse::New and Collected Poems
Description: First Edition. | Bailey: Motina Books, 2024

Identifiers:

LCCN: 2026932749

ISBN-13: 979-8-88784-073-4 (paperback)
ISBN-13: 979-8-88784-074-1 (hardcover)

Subjects: BISAC:
POETRY / American / General

Cover art by Erin Needham

For My son, Matthew, and his mother, my wife Jane, my sister, Marie, my brother, Leonard Wayne and my beloved nieces and nephews

Praise for *Somewhere There's a Horse*

"*Somewhere There's a Horse* is Ron Wallace at his meditative best. Time is his recurring theme, yet each poem finds a new angle on aging, a new image in old memories cutting to the heart of the matter. And when meditation won't do, Wallace isn't scared to wrestle with his subject like a late summer storm, determined to *rage and roll on / with days growing shorter / and time winding down*."

~ Cullen Whisenhunt,
Author of *Until Air Itself Is Tinted*
Winner of the 2024 Oklahoma Book
Award for Poetry

"To paraphrase Whitman: The poet's gift to his reader is to fill him with good heart. Ron Wallace delivers that gift on every page of *Somewhere There's a Horse*. If you seek important things, long-lasting things: Integrity, Dignity, Hope, Courage, Identity, Humanity — well then, don't waste another moment; accept Wallace's gift and read *Somewhere There's a Horse*.

~ Chuck Ladd
Author of *A Quiet Place in Oklahoma*

"Wallace's poems begin solidly in good Oklahoma dirt, journey to the Wichitas, to Colorado, to Wyoming, and the wild ghosts of the West, then explode into the heavens. In his poem, 'The Depth and Distance of February,' one of my all-time favorite titles EVER, he evokes a mourning 'sadder than the bluest notes from an old Hank Williams song' and should strike the reader wanting to keep this book close at hand, like a memory."

~Sandra Soli
author of *What Trees Know*
Winner of 2008 Oklahoma Book Award

"You don't just wake up one morning and discover that you are magically a widely admired, multi-award-winning poet. You have to have lived the life required and put in the work necessary to get to that point.

Ron Wallace checks all the boxes, and this new collection. *Somewhere There's a Horse*, will solidify his position near the top of poets of the Southwest.

These are winter poems with all that implies: aging, survival, memories, longing. Yet the reader will come out at the end of this book as a stronger, braver person. It takes an amazing poet to accomplish that."

~Bill McCloud
author of *The Error of the Stars*
Silence Dogood Books

INTRODUCTION

These poems in Ron Wallace's latest collection are the musings of a man trying to reckon how best to make peace with mortality as he looks ahead to the inevitable end of his calendar days.

The poet's voice is that of a born and bred Oklahoman. His Okie accent is steeped in the lore of the old cowboy West—plain talk made melodious with language and resonances from a life of reading, teaching and writing poetry.

The first stanza of the opening poem is a good example of the poet's singular voice:

Demember is a gunslinger
        with Eastwood eyes
                standing at the end of the bar,
a shot glass full of whiskey in his left hand,
his right perilously near a .44
        strapped on his hip
                tethered to his leg.
He's come to try me once again.

Wallace's is a voice that ranges from the elegiac to the celebratory — a voice in search of wisdom from anywhere it can be found, from the earth to the sky, the planet to the cosmos. From the everyday to the spiritual. A voice of someone unafraid to get mud on his boots or to marvel at the sight of a hawk as it leaves its perch to fly off toward the unseen horizon of the sky.

Nor is the poet afraid to declare the simple memory of himself and a long-time friend playing a game of catch in their early seventies as:

the holiest of sacraments
      that is calling us
to receive the consecration of lost youth

In the closing lines of "Gunslinger", the poet reminds us, by reminding himself via Robert Frost, that we have "miles to go and promises to keep" before we leave.

This is a book worthy of your time. Read it.

Paul Austin
Author of *Mother and Son*
2025 Turning Plow Press

TEN TOUCHSTONES TO PONDER
BEFORE READING

I believe poetry happens to the poet before the poet ever writes it, sometimes long before, and I am relatively certain that most poets would affirm this if they were ever asked.

The writers who have affected me, moved me, made me, shaped me; be they prose, poetry, or songwriters have all taught me valuable lessons

I always stress to emerging writers that to be good at what they wish to do requires exposure to the greatness of other writers. If one does not read the words of great authors, listen to the powerful lyrics of the masters and think deeply about what they have encountered, how can they feel the depth and voice needed to create their own work.

A poet may not be Shakespeare, but if they listen, they can find their own voice, their own heart like the voices below have found theirs. They can become themselves and grow into who they are meant to be.

"What is life? It is the flash of a firefly in the night. It is the breath of a buffalo in wintertime. It is the little shadow which runs across the grass and loses itself in the sunset.

~ Crowfoot

"Poetry is just the evidence of life. If your life is burning well, poetry is just the ash."

~ Leonard Cohen

"The act of writing requires a constant plunging back into the shadow of the past where time hovers ghostlike."

~ Ralph Ellison

"The years go by like days; sometimes the days go by like years, and I don't know which one I hate the most."
          ~ Gretchen Peters

"You've got to heal faster than those bastards can hurt you."
          ~ Chris Wall

"I am a series of small victories and large defeats, and I am amazed as any other that I have gotten from there to here."
          ~ Charles Bukowski

"I did not know then how much had ended."
          ~ Black Elk

"Now the things that I remember seem so distant and so small, though it really hasn't been that long a time. What I was seeing wasn't what was happening at all. "
          ~ Jackson Browne

"Parting is all we know of Heaven and all we need of Hell."
          ~ Emily Dickinson

"Breathe in, breathe out, move on."
          ~ Jimmy Buffett

GUNSLINGER

December is a gunslinger
    with Eastwood eyes
        standing at the end of the bar,
a shot glass full of whiskey in his left hand,
his right perilously near a .44
    strapped on his hip
        tethered to his leg.
He's come to try me once again.

I know him well.
I've faced him often.

There was a time
back before his outlaw days.
    when we   almost
could have been considered friends.
He wasn't so quick back then,
seems I always beat him on the draw,
    and our time together
passed without animosity or anger.
But, these are different days.
    I think he's faster.
        I know I'm slower.
Still, I'm not done.
I can clear leather before he does
    even if
it's only… by half a thunderclap.

So those woods,
    lovely, dark, and deep
will have to wait,
for as my Yankee poet friend once said,
"I have promises to keep
and miles to go before I sleep."

SOMEWHERE THERE'S A HORSE

The old man was sitting alone at the bar
     his back to me
at a Denny's Restaurant
in Raton, New Mexico.
Tourists headed north for Colorado
     coming in for breakfast
paid him no more notice
than the pinon pines they'd just driven past.

He was built
thin and tough as a barbed wire fence.
His faded Levi blue jean jacket
     worn thin at the elbows
        looked like it came from 1962,
and his Wrangler jeans
were probably older than his waitress.
His cowboy hat,
a Stetson, I'm sure,
     once cream-colored
        now sweat-stained
was curled a little on one side
from too many years of pulling it down snug
against New Mexico winds.

It was only
     when he rose
and stepped down from his stool
that I noticed the grimace
as he wavered
     seeking balance
on the worn heels of his scuffed boots.

"Are you okay?"
the young waitress asked
true concern in her small voice.
He nodded,
        "Just a little dizzy spell."

But as he turned
and placed a twenty-dollar bill
down on the bar
        I saw the look,
the dread and determination
                a silent pleading
                        in faded grey eyes
that said only to himself,
"No, not here.
Not in a goddamned Denny's."

Then slowly he placed one foot
        ahead of the next
just like a cowboy is supposed to do
until he stepped out
into the cool Sangre de Cristo Mountain air,

where, somewhere, I knew, there was a horse.

CONSECRATION
(for Mike Bush)

Waiting on our foursome to manifest
and golf to happen
      we see the gloves,
my Wilson A2000 (fifty years old)
and a black Rawlings Ricky Henderson model,
my son's glove
      both accumulating dust
         on a shelf
            in the garage.
They call to us in hymnlike incantations,
asking to be lifted up
      and dusted off
with fists popping into the pockets.
A well-worn baseball is resting
wrapped in the leather
of the A2000
and we have tattered remnants
      of time to kill.

Mike is 70 and I am 71;
we know well the holiest of sacraments
      that is calling us
to receive the consecration of lost youth,
so we separate at twenty feet
      not ninety anymore,
and with a creak of shoulder and wrists
I deliver the first toss of the ball with a soft arc
      toward my old infield partner.
He gloves it with natural ease
and returns it with the same gentle arc
      flexing his right arm
after this first communion of flight.

With each throw
years melt into the magic of music
        horsehide and leather
playing a concert over sixty years in the making,
no longer carrying the notes
of gloves singing
        with rifle fire
but instead a softer hum revealing
that the silk of ten thousand throws
        ten thousand catches
has not frayed the fabric of time enough
to stop the song.

RUSTLER

September solstice,
autumn's lead steer eases out
     ahead of the herd,
moving at its own slow, sullen pace
toward the railhead
     of a distant spring.

Lightning burns the western sky
     like a cattle brand
          on the hip of October,
searing the season's end,
marking the night
with a single flash of fire-white light.

Winter is a rustler
     with a running iron
in his cold and calloused hand.
The freeze will follow
chilling the air in our lungs,
and January will bend his black brim
down a little lower
     strike a starlit cigarette
and blow summer in a smoke ring
up into a grey and vacant sky.

OF HORSES AND HAWKS
AND ALL THINGS IN BETWEEN

The morning sun is painting June
     on a blue-sky canvas
with slashing strokes of cirrus clouds
above the gathering greens of hickory
     and pecan trees,
guarding the eastern edge of pasture grass.

Another summer is being shaped
     in rising spirals
          of a redtail hawk
above a wicked twist of shallow river
where four horses emerge
from the mist along the muddy banks
as if being born
     from the earth itself.

This is my Oklahoma,
a locus of horse
     hawk
and all things that live between,
a painting
hung by a single strand
of antique barbed wire
on gnarled bois d'arc fence posts,
anchoring the world to the coming day.

Look on my Works, ye Mighty, and despair!
Percy Bysshe Shelley

WEST TEXAS OZYMANDIAS

Traveling West Texas,
on a stretch of panhandle highway
west of Matador
     I saw a hawk
perched on the crucifix of a highline pole
a pewter sky behind him,
his eyes, fixed on the remnants
of what might have been a church
or maybe a school,
now only a rubble of iron and bricks
     tangled in vines.
One unroofed corner of crumbling walls
remaining among the tumbled stones
     VICTORY
carved in a granite lintel above a damaged doorway.

I slowed the Jeep
to look.
On the Plains before me,
     nothing but mesquite
          and windswept sand stretched out
             toward New Mexico.
The road around me had fallen silent.
Not a creature stirred
until I put the ruin in my rearview mirror
and watched the hawk rise
     high above the desolation
        into the sun.

EMPTY

A wolf moon
hangs in the January night
     indigo blue
with a scatter of stars spilling around it.

Outside
I stand below its light
in the ink black shadow of trees
     shrouded in darkness,
no light coming
from the darkened windows.

And I listen
listen for a single cricket's song
     or a coyote's howl,
maybe the wind rattling the branches above,
but there is simply no sound
     only silence
          in an empty world.

PAINTING SUPERMAN

It may be
the only photo of Dad with me as a boy
      not a baby
      not a man
not a near man but as a little boy.

My sister-in-law, Linda says, "Look up."
      and we do.
My eyes cutting away
from the paint-by-numbers Superman
      I look up
into the lens of a distant day
that only one of us will ever see.

It is 1965,
      my twelfth birthday
The remnants of a cake that Momma made
is on the table before us
and Dad's eyes have followed mine
      peering above his glasses
and the pages of the Durant Daily Democrat
to the magic held in Linda's hands.

Even in the black and white
of six decades
I still see the bright blues of Superman's suit
      the bold, red "S"
in a yellow pentagon emblazoned on his chest,
the scarlet cape
      flowing from his shoulders,
the paper muscles rippling
beneath the bright colors I am painting.

Six decades
stacked on my shoulders now
and, I can see what I could not see in 1965,
        real muscles
flexing from the sleeves seated beside me,
muscles made by sixty years
of swinging a steel horseshoe hammer
        lifting fifty-pound feed bags
                manhandling contrary livestock,
muscles made by hard work in hard times,
muscles impervious to Kryptonite.

Too late, I have learned
Superman wasn't on that paint-by-numbers
cardboard canvas.
Instead, he was sitting right there
        next to me,
        reading his newspaper,
        peering over Clark Kent glasses.

SIXTY FEET, SIX INCHES

I remember when
Home lay exactly sixty feet six inches away
embedded firmly in red clay
      so close
that I could almost reach down
and touch it.
I could peer
      from a mound of dirt
into days that would never fade nor fail.

Now,
seven decades done
      looking out from a mist
that same sixty feet, six inches has fallen away,

Home
      stretching
           too far a distance to cover
with the flight of a horsehide sphere.
All I can see
is a scattering of ashes
dancing in a December wind,
a blur of blue years
      and a murder of crows cackling
         at a joke
that I somehow must have missed.

AVOIDING TIGERS

An Oklahoma ghost moon
hangs in the pale blue
above the concrete ribbon unfurling
     before me,
with the threat of December grey
emerging from leafless trees.

On days like these
     I often fail to find
the hawk who guides me.
No pathways open before my eyes
     no trails appear
through the forest, dark and filled
with emptiness.

These are the days
I sense Bukowski's Tigers stalking me
herding me toward the shadows
     where they live.
These days sing sorrow on sad notes
of soft wind
through the trees.

I do not like these days.

SENTRY

In mottled feathers of browns and greys,
the great horned owl
became invisible,
sitting in the dusky light of owls
among the limbs of oaks and elms
mottled just as brown and grey as he.

"Who, who", comes the sentry's call,
revealing his presence
as I stand beneath the barren branches
in this little cemetery
where my fallen shepherd lies
in his plot next to the bones of beloved cats.

"Just me," I answer,
"Come to talk with a few old ghosts a while."

Then a rush of sudden air
the lift of invisible wings in flight
gathering up the last light,
acknowledging a sentry's acceptance
of my feet on hallowed grounds
beneath his star-shrouded skies.

SCUFFED

Sometimes my soul
feels as worn and scuffed as my old boots.
There are days
I feel every scar cut into the leather
      every broken stitch
in the quarters and crown,
the uneven wear of the cowboy heels
      that has changed my gait
with an inward bent to each foot.

I no longer step from the stirrup
in full stride
but move with a bowlegged amble,
kicking off the cowshit
      on an uphill path
past the gates of autumn and
into winter's corral.

ALL THINGS BURN

All things burn,
and in the confusion and calculation of fire
     we believe in the blaze,
its dancing in the darkness,
burning night
into a dazzling light,
the Promethean intensity of life
     mingling
with a godlike power of destruction
and a marvel of beauty
     holding us fast,
not unlike those Olympian chains
that bound the Titan
     to the rock.

But for all our faith,
we can no more hold the flame
than the smoke
     rising in curls
dissipating above ember and ash.

We are left
with fading memory
     an essence
that steals the air we breathe
before fading into nothingness
     as we, too
        burn.

SCATTERING THE ASHES

(10/12/2025)

Five brothers,
we once stalked this terrain
like panthers.
This was our yard;
its ground and grass we ran
from the break of day
      until dark.
Now
it is almost unrecognizable.
Trees grow where walls and windows
stood before.
Old elms have collapsed,
and doorways to Christmases
      Thanksgivings
Easters and birthdays past
have slammed closed
      in a circling of suns,
but we have returned,
      four of us
in flesh, one in ashes to be scattered.
We know
that you are not these ashes that we carry.
They are only the empty remnants
of a body you once lived in
      a body,
we knew well before you flew away.
We come here,
here to this place from which we all sprung
merely to unsheathe your mortality
      to allow it to mingle
with ashes of this fallen home
until we become
      five again.

"Feeling nearly faded as my jeans"
Kris Kristofferson

COYOTE BONES AND WOODEN CROSSES

October moves
down a concrete river
across the Southern Plains of Oklahoma
      west of Waurika,
          July dry and August hot.
"Me and Bobby McGee" playing
on the radio,
a fifty-nine Ford rusting
      next to a house
where no one lives anymore,
where no one can hear the air singing.

Freedom's just another word for
nothin' left to lose.

The miles pour through the autumn windshield
on this long stretch
      of nothing
          to nowhere
until my eyes find
the broken bones of a coyote carcass
      lying in dry grass
next to a weathered wooden cross,
beside a barbed wire fence

What once might have been a name,
        is gone
                faded
like the plastic flowers falling
from the marker's embrace
        down to dirt
that has become all too familiar
with death
and bois d'arc fence posts
        holding up
only barbed wire and blue sky.

And I fly past
        New Mexico bound
my tires humming on the lonely blacktop
the vacant air singing…

Nothin' ain't worth nothin'
        but it's free

Devouring time, blunt thou the lion's paws.
William Shakespeare

LIFTING WEIGHTS

I am an Oklahoman.
I became a weightlifter early
        a mover of all things heavy.
With my people
carrying the ballast became second nature.
        From my youth,
it seemed my legs and back were built
to lift a load and bear a burden.
        I grew strong
like my father, brothers and uncles,
but no one warned me of weights
        that would, one day, come.

On the day that I lifted my father
        fallen
from the inevitable gravity of winter,
I was not ready for his lightness of being,
        the want of any real heft.
He should have been a massive hulk
not the mere husk of a man
        not the pale shadow,
that I lifted from the wooden floor
featherlight as a child.

I discovered, then, that weight
is not always measured in pounds
        No, the heaviest weight
is measured in days,
heavier than any steel or stone
        could ever be.

SOME SINS

Mistakes,
I've made more than my share;
too much damage
I have done,
but I don't seek forgiveness
        nor do I ask absolution.
I'll wear my wrongs
like scars
or blue tattoos
etched upon my heart
        hidden
beneath a faded denim shirt.

They belong to me
        and no one else.
I made them
and in return they made me.

I promise
you will never hear me say
        "If only
I could do it all over again
if only, I had another chance
        I wouldn't change a thing."

No, there are things
not that many, but a few, I'd gladly change.
But there will always be
some failings I cannot release,
        some hurts
I can never heal.

There are some sins that I must keep.

HOUSE

Once,
my home stood right here
      in the shade of chinaberry trees
      a massive elm,
and a tall cottonwood towering
above bright green Bermuda blades.
Pansies and petunias
      four o'clocks
      and the little blue blossoms
whose names I never knew
grew next to Mama's roses
just outside my rusting window screen.
But that was a long, long time ago.

After the fire,
I returned
      to find a fraction
of my old bedroom wall still standing
among the rubble
like a shard of shattered glass
      in a broken windowpane.
I saw the flowering purple crepe myrtle
singed and bare,
and I cursed the gift of Prometheus.

Years later
      the ash and the rubble gone,
I am drawn again to this emptiness.
The cement walkway
leading from the shortest street
      in our town
up to the concrete front porch
is all that remains
to testify that a house was ever here.

My boots kick the dirt
        away from a red brick,
buried in pine needles
before my eyes lift to the cry of a hawk
circling above the silence.

Sunlight shifts
through a tangle of trees
        deceiving reality
                creating an illusion
of movement in the shadows
as if somehow
the Sunday ghosts
might be gathering in the kitchen,
and I can almost feel the laughter
vibrating off fallen walls
which once held our lives and our faces
        hanging in photographs
or balanced precariously
on wooden, shop-class, whatnot shelves,
now etched in September air
        unburnable.
And just for a moment
        all the gods that may be,
                except Chronos
                        are forgiven.

A LACK OF ELOQUENCE

Why is life
    so damned often
        inarticulate?

Life should be eloquent poetry
    Shakespeare
        or maybe Whitman
singing with the sweet sound
of Linda Ronstadt
or the raspy growl of Kristofferson.
    It should laugh
like Jimmy Buffett,
cry like Johnny Cash or Hank Williams.
Life should flow,
with the melodic, vibrant Southern baritone
    of Dr. King
or echo with the Yankee twang of JFK.
Life should bring us wisdom
    sounding like Solomon
        or Einstein,
Aristotle or Socrates.

Hell…
I might even settle for George Carlin's
sharp sarcastic wit.

But, oh no,
too often, it rambles on,
    stammers and stumbles,
sounding more like
a drunken, tongue-tied Georgia hillbilly
with an IQ of eighty-two…
    just so damned
        inarticulate.

THE WEIGHT OF HORSEHIDE

I have grown old
throwing a baseball.
But I know the lightness of being
    that is borne
in a throwing arm as it hefts
a five and a quarter ounce horsehide sphere.

My fingertips feel the kinship to leather
and raised red threads
    that stitch past to present
like a tailor's needle
fastening an elemental fabric of the heart
to the hand.

I still carry my glove into the sun
    holding a baseball
to be thrown
over an ever-shrinking distance
across space and time,

for I know the sacrament received
on its return,
the turning of two into one
    the welding of souls
        the lifting of burdens
bringing a moment's peace,
warmth
to a world sheathed in cold chaos.

OKLAHOMA ACCENTS

I'm told
I speak with an Oklahoma accent.
Most folks say
that when I unhorse a participle phrase,
it rolls through prairie grass and under fences
     like a wolf stalking prey.
My subjects and my verbs will occasionally disagree.
Even my adverbs all wear cowboy hats,
     brims pulled low,
with dark mustaches drooping down over adjectives.
And I don't mean to brag
     but in midsentence,
I can draw a double negative,
twirl it like a .44 on my finger
     and reholster it
before anyone even knows that it was spoken.
I tend to reckon
more than I think or believe,
     and "ain't"
     "ain't" just fits me to a T
like a good pair of boots fits a man's feet.
Sometimes my voice may rumble low,
 a horse herd in the distance,
     but with just a touch of spur,
I can summon up a stampede if I need it.

Yep, so far,
over my seven decades on this little rock,
     it hasn't been that much a problem.
When I carry on a conversation with my Maker,
I speak with that same Okie accent,
and He seems to get every single syllable.

Why just last night
over a couple of good cold beers
        I laughed and said,
"You know, Man,
I don't get most of this religious shit."
        And He laughed right back
and opened up another beer.
"Y'all ain't got nuthin' to worry about, Bud.
The shit's all theirs.
        Ain't none of it mine.
Hell,
I don't get much of it most of the time, myself.

Some good ol' boys
made up about half of all that.
I really only got one rule to go by:
        Treat all folks,
        and I do mean all,
the way that they deserve,
the way you'd have 'em treatin' you
if the boot was on the other foot."

I took a long drink and thought,
Huh!
Come to think of it
God's got an Okie accent too.

At least He does when He talks to me.

CROSSING

Here,
far out on the Plains
    I am driving
near seventy-five miles an hour
across an August Oklahoma Panhandle
where two hundred years ago,
warriors of the Southern Cheyenne,
maybe Yellow Wolf
    or Black Kettle,
descended from what is now Kansas and Colorado
following the great herds of shaggy bison
    across vast grasslands.

But those days have disappeared
    like the buffalo they once pursued.

Now
only a twenty-five-foot-high wooden windmill
    a postcard image of western days
spins its rough-cut, tin blades
near a few tame
    scattered cattle
wandering this low roll of land
fenced off
by barbed wire and Oklahoma Highway 3,
kept apart from the spinning giants
that have taken the prairie.

These metal beasts
like titans stand over everything
        whirling the air,
above this trail of concrete and steel
 that is carrying me away
far away from a fading past
        away from the ghosts of buffalo
and Southern Cheyenne warriors
across the Canadian
        over the Washita
                and toward the Red,
toward the twenty-first century and home.

ANACHRONISM

The end of summer air
    smells like rain
and lightning jags in the looming blackness
miles to the west.
But here,
the flames of the sun
fling our shadow onto black asphalt
as we roll toward the storm.

What pass as mountains in Oklahoma
    the Wichitas
stand above grasslands
where an ancient bull buffalo grazing
among clumps of Indian grass
    lifts his shaggy head
to glare at a metal beast as blue as sky
rolling past him, violating his piece of earth.

And for a moment,
we seem more the anachronism here
    than he is
as we race past
toward a winding highway 54
that will carry us to Gotebo
    Cloud Chief
and eventually to Clinton
on what was once called the Mother Road,
swallowed now by I-40
    devoid of all roadside bison.

STORM

In the last days of August,
black clouds
gathering in the southeast
     surge ---
the rounded humps and short horns
of stampeding bison
purpling the dark slate grey
     like an angry bruise.

Lightning,
buried deep in the coming black
     leaps to earth
         burning
the dusk, white in a flash
before disappearing.

This is as it should be.

Summer should never surrender
     too quietly,
never fold itself neatly into fall.

Let it bring the crash of thunder
this rumbling herd of buffalo,
     let lightning split the oak
         hailstones pelt the ground,
and rain paint the air
black as fury
Let the season's ending rage and roll on
     with days growing shorter
         and time winding down.

DINOSAUR

It's not easy being a curved cap bill
      in a sea full of flat ones,
a pair of round-toed boots among the square,
a being bordering on extinction
      trying to function
in a confusing, fucked-up world.

Some days, I dream
I have fallen through lost CDs,
discarded cassettes
      and VCR tapes
only to land in the midst of Hoyt Axton,
CCR and Three Dog Night
      piled in a heap
of broken eight tracks.

I rise,
half expecting to find my footprints
      pressed into the detritus
of books by Steinbeck or Whitman's poetry,
preserved in a museum
as evidence that once we read
      turned actual pages,
where Tom Joad, Owen Meany,
and Augustus McCrae
sat on antique, oaken shelves
      undigitalized.

THE DEPTH AND DISTANCE
OF FEBRUARY

If I were a Redtail hawk
        I'd unfurl my wings
and fly into a cloudless blue,
ride the air
in ever-widening spirals,
wrapped in coldest sunlight
        high above
the depth and distance of February.

But I am a man,
mortal, a prisoner of featherless bones
        more prey than predator
fastened firmly
to a slow-turning earth
where I hear winter singing holy, holy
        oh, so goddamned holy
through the bare and leafless trees,
sadder than the bluest notes
of an old Hank Williams song.

OUTLAW

Is this weather a blessing
or a curse?
The sky above is overcast
      in shades of slate grey,
and an unexpected cool mist has drowned
the sweltering heat.

This outlaw air
has stolen the sun from an unbranded sky
      like a cattle rustler,
riding in the darkness
out of Kiowa County Colorado in 1880.
Summer must have failed to set a watchman
or some magic mischief is at hand.
What's next?
      October snow
           or a January hurricane?

This cannot be right.
I should be seeking shade after sweating
behind a power mower,
not feeling a breeze cool as December
on my skin,
moving blackened clouds
      west to east
           threatening rain
in the depths
of an Oklahoma August afternoon.

IT MATTERS NOT

On warm October nights
when the full moon shines bright
the ghost of a half-black Kiowa outlaw
  can be seen
crossing Red River
to meet a Gypsy shadow,
  waiting
beneath a field of Oklahoma stars
that have slipped silently
  into a Texas sky.

It matters not
to that moon nor those ornamental stars
why these two are there
  It matters not
that she wears his name tattooed in blue
above her beating heart
  nor that he his drawn
like the damned into the flames.

It only matters
to a world that they did not create
a world where rules and laws
  are born in hate.

DEATH OF A POETIC MASTERPIECE

There was a blood stain on the margins
of the first draft.
What the hell happened
        to this alleged poem?
Its body seemed strong,
filled with poetic thoughts, original metaphors
        free of cliched similes
                damned near Whitmanesque,
not a cicada in it to trouble Billy Collins.

Then bam!
All intellect and beauty were slaughtered
        like extras
in a Quentin Tarantino film,
its dismembered corpse tossed in the trunk
of an abandoned '76 AMC Gremlin.

Rumors hinted
some elaborate, cartel money-laundering scheme
was involved,
        but those didn't last long;
we all knew it was impossible.
If it had really been a poem,
money could not have been involved,
not dirty money,
        not clean money
                not even pocket change.

Any trace of Starks, Dickey, Fairchild, or Jeffers
was sought to no avail.
Juhasz, Whisenhunt, Austin, Hada and Hank Jones
        were quickly consulted.
Ben Myers and Markham Johnson,
Chuck Ladd, Jim Fletcher, and Bill McCloud.
        Alan Berecka

Nathan Brown
Paul Bowers
Tom Murphy, Phil Morgan and Lance Henson
all were called
      but the crime remained a mystery.

Seeking different perspectives
      other angles
            sharper minds
the cry went out
to Carol Hamilton and Sandra Soli
Chappell, Chafins, Isaacs and Joey Brown
      Sharon Martin
            Judith Rycroft
                  Ky George.

"We need Larry Thomas,"
      came the consensus,
but the buffalo had gone off to New Mexico.

"What about Billy Collins," someone said.
      "Way too Yankee,
for this Southern shit," came a muffled voice
from somewhere in the pack.

Finally, in desperation, we held a séance
seeking the ghosts
of Walt Whitman,
Dorothy Alexander and Jim Spurr,
but what happened to this almost-a-poem
      still, no one knew.

Desperation was setting in.

A posse was dispatched
in search of the legendary Ray Wylie Hubbard
who was playing at a bar in Soper.
The man who wrote "Up Against the Wall

Redneck Mother"
        "Snake Farm",
and "Conversation with the Devil"
was bound to have the answer.

But, alas…
        in the end,
even Ray Wylie was confounded.
He simply strummed his Gold Top Les Paul
        looked up and said,
"Some get spiritual 'cause they see the light
and some 'cause they feel the heat."

"What the hell does that mean?"
        we all asked in unison.
But Ray just grinned and said,
"Only two people I know might have a clue:
        Willie Nelson
                and Woodstock Farley,
and you're in luck;
Woodstock's parked out back
        lightin' one up on the bus."

Woodstock sat barefooted
in the lotus position,
and inhaled deeply
as he pondered the surviving manuscript.
        He blew a smoke ring
into the air and spoke with a graveled voice,

"I've read whatever this is several times now,
and the only practicable conclusion is:
         that too much sentiment crept in,
some hackneyed cliché infiltrated the stanzas,
slipping through the white space
         like…
         like a thief in the night
         and as quick as a blink
unraveled the iambic pentameter,
injected it with an overdose
of maudlin prose
before finally clubbing the work in the head
         with a hidden haiku,
                  leaving it for dead.
There's nothing that can be done to save it, now.
Give it a decent burial,
or better yet a warrior's cremation,"
he said, igniting the paper
with the glowing end of his honey blunt.

Amazed,
breathing in his wisdom
we peered through the gathering cloud of smoke
         at the shaman in a surfer shirt
and collectively exhaled.

"Of course," we all echoed.
"It was just too damned obvious."

NOTES

"Sixty Feet, Six Inches" first appeared in eMerge Magazine – September 2025

"Somewhere There's a Horse", "Empty", and "Of Hawks, Horses and All Things in Between" first appeared in Dos Gatos Magazine – November 2025

ABOUT THE AUTHOR

Ron Wallace is an Oklahoma native and currently an adjunct instructor of Literature and Composition, at Southeastern Oklahoma State University, in Durant. He is the author of twelve books of poetry, five of which have been finalists in the Oklahoma Book Awards with *Renegade and Other Poems* winning the 2018 award.

Wallace has been a multiple "Pushcart Prize" nominee and has recently been published in "Oklahoma Today," "Dos gatos Magazine," "eMerge Magazine," and a number of other magazines. He has also written his first novel *A Secret Lies in New Orleans* which was a finalist in fiction in the 2022 Oklahoma Book Awards.